# FEBRUARY

## A MONTH OF REPRODUCIBLES AT YOUR FINGERTIPS!

**Grade 1**

**Editor:**
Susan Hohbach Walker

**Writers:**
Amy Erickson, Sharon Murphy,
Susan Hohbach Walker

**Art Coordinator:**
Clevell Harris

**Artists:**
Jennifer Tipton Bennett, Cathy Spangler Bruce,
Nick Greenwood, Clevell Harris,
Sheila Krill, Rob Mayworth

**Cover Artist:**
Jennifer Tipton Bennett

www.themailbox.com

©1998 by THE EDUCATION CENTER, INC.
All rights reserved.
ISBN #1-56234-222-3

Manufactured in the United States

10 9 8 7 6 5 4 3 2

# Table Of Contents

Name

# February Calendar Capers

| Monday | Tuesday | Wednesday | Thursday | Friday |
|---|---|---|---|---|
| February is Responsible Pet Owner Month. Discuss with students why pets are important to us and how pets depend on their owners for certain needs. | February 2 is Groundhog Day. Take students outside to look for their shadows. | February is Canned Food Month. Have students donate canned goods to a local soup kitchen or food pantry. | On February 5 celebrate the date that the Wiffle® ball was first sold. Explain that the Wiffle® ball has holes in order to lessen the distance it will travel. During free time, have several Wiffle® balls and rubber balls available for students to use. | Celebrate the birthdate of Laura Ingalls Wilder on February 7 by reading aloud *Winter Days In The Big Woods* from the series My First Little House Books (Scholastic Inc.). |
| National Pancake Week is observed the week of *Shrove* or *Pancake Tuesday* (the day before Ash Wednesday). Recruit parent volunteers to treat your students to a pancake breakfast during the week. | In honor of Potato Lovers Month, have students name their favorite ways to eat a potato. | Celebrate the birthdate of Thomas Edison, developer of the lightbulb, on February 11. Discuss with students the importance of his invention. | The second Wednesday in February is Lost Penny Day. Have students collect extra pennies from home and give them to a shelter or local Humane Society. | Valentine's Day is February 14. Have each child create a card for a friend or family member.  |
| The third Monday in February is Presidents' Day. This day recognizes the birthdays of George Washington and Abraham Lincoln. Have students sing "Happy Birthday" in honor of these presidents. | February is National Wild Bird–Feeding Month. Encourage students to make bird feeders by spreading peanut butter on pinecones and then rolling the pinecones in sunflower seeds. | George Washington's meals often had eight meat dishes! Have each child describe the biggest meal he has ever eaten. | February 16 is Heart 2 Heart Day—a day to encourage diary writing. Have students use journal writing as a means of expressing themselves. Provide time each day for your students to write in their journals. | February 20 is Student Volunteer Day. Invite students to brainstorm specific ways they can volunteer in the school or community.  |
| National Pencil Week is celebrated during the last full week of February. Have each child write a story titled "A Day In The Life Of My Pencil." | The first telephone directory was issued in New Haven, Connecticut, on February 21, 1878. It had only 50 listings. Show students a phone book from your community and demonstrate how to look for specific listings. | February 26 is the birthdate of Levi Strauss—the creator of the first pair of jeans. Invite students to wear something made of denim today. | February 28 is Floral Design Day. Have each student draw a bouquet of flowers. | Leap year gives February a 29th day every four years. Ask students how they would feel if their birthdays were on February 29 and only came every four years.  |

©1998 The Education Center, Inc. • *February Monthly Reproducibles* • Grade 1 • TEC940

**Note To The Teacher:** Highlight special days and events with these fact-filled ideas.

3

# FEBRUARY
## Events And Activities For The Family

**Directions:** Select at least one activity below to complete as a family by the end of February.
*(Challenge: See if your family can complete all three activities.)*

### Groundhog Day

When will winter weather end? Punxsutawney Phil allegedly answers this question each year on February 2. According to legend, if this groundhog sees his shadow, six more weeks of winter are in store for us. If he doesn't, spring is just around the corner!

Celebrate this day with your family by creating shadow pictures. Demonstrate how to make a shadow by holding your hand between a light source and a wall. Then have your children experiment with hand shadows. Can your youngsters make their shadows smaller? Larger? Challenge them to make hand shadows that resemble creatures, such as ducks, horses, and dogs. Hands down, this shadow play will delight your students!

### Valentine's Day

In honor of this holiday on February 14, help your youngsters make adorable handmade decorations. In no time at all, this simple Valentine's Day project will be ready for gift giving or for displaying in your own home!

**A Divine Valentine**

**Materials For One Decoration:**
1 frozen juice can lid
1 paper doily
two 7" lengths of narrow ribbon
1 small piece of decorative Con-Tact® paper
construction-paper scraps
scissors
craft glue

**Directions:**
1. Cut out a Con-Tact® paper circle to fit within the rim on the top side of the lid. Peel off the backing and adhere the circle to the lid.
2. Cut out and glue small construction-paper hearts to decorate the Con-Tact® paper circle.
3. Knot a length of ribbon to make a hanger. Glue it to the back of the lid as shown.
4. Glue the back of the lid in the center of the doily.
5. Tie a bow with the second length of ribbon and glue it; then set aside the resulting decoration to dry.

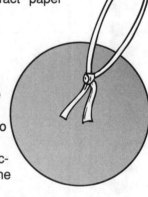

### Fairy Tales

Recognize Wilhelm Grimm's birthday on February 24 by creating a unique family fairy tale. Long ago fairy tales were passed from generation to generation with oral retellings. Grimm and his brother published many of these delightful tales to ensure that they were preserved.

Choose one family member to start telling an original fairy tale. After a few minutes, have him or her stop, and ask the next person to continue the story. For added fun, a turn may end at a suspenseful moment in the story or even mid-sentence! This activity is sure to spark youngsters' imaginations and it's perfect entertainment for long family trips.

**Note To The Teacher:** Distribute one copy of this reproducible to each student at the beginning of the month. Encourage each family to complete at least one activity by the end of February.

# GROUNDHOG DAY

It's February 2! Will the groundhog see his shadow or won't he? This basic question—as legend has it—determines spring's arrival. Groundhog Day celebrates the belief that if the sun shines on Candlemas Day, or if the groundhog sees his shadow on this day, there will be six more weeks of winter. Punxsutawney, Pennsylvania, is famous for Punxsutawney Phil—a groundhog well-known for his annual weather prediction.

## Punxsutawney Predictions

Predicting and graphing skills are necessary to complete this interesting activity.
On a day prior to Groundhog Day, have each child predict whether or not the groundhog will see his shadow. Have students record their predictions on a chart as shown. Watch weather reports on February 2 to see how many predictions were right. Then have students record daily temperatures for the six weeks following Groundhog Day to see if Phil's prediction was accurate, too.

| Groundhog **will** see his shadow. | Groundhog **won't** see his shadow. |
| --- | --- |
| John J. | Teresa |
| DeDe | Rob |
| Sue | Pam |
| Sam | Nick |
| | Mary |
| | Andy |
| | Maggie |
| | Bert |
| | LaTonya |
| | Shantel |
| | Kevin |
| | Todd |
| | Jessie |

## More Winter! Now What?

Did the groundhog see his shadow this year? Don't let winter get your students down. Try this fun activity to bring a little springtime to your classroom. Cut a length of bulletin-board paper for a class-created mural. Have each child color images of spring (flowers, grass, butterflies, trees, etc.). To complete the mural, give each child an artificial flower to add to the mural. Tape the flowers among those that were drawn. These three-dimensional additions make the mural especially attractive and will really bring spring to life in your classroom—despite the chilly air outside.

# Shadow Story

Read the story.

Was it time for spring? All the animals were waiting to find out. Where was Mr. Groundhog? He would decide if spring would come or if there would be more winter.

All the animals called for Mr. Groundhog. Soon he poked his nose through the dirt. Mr. Groundhog pulled himself from the hole. He did not see his shadow. "Hooray!" the animals shouted. "It is time for spring!"

Answer the questions.

1.  Who would decide if spring would start?

    _____

    _____

2.  Where did Mr. Groundhog live?

    _____

    _____

3.  What was Mr. Groundhog looking for?

    _____

    _____

4.  How did the animals feel at the end of the story?

    _____

    _____

**Bonus Box:** Draw clouds in the sky to hide the sun.

Name _____

# Thinkin' About Vowels

Name each picture.
Circle the vowel sound.

| | | | |
|---|---|---|---|
| a  e  u | e  i  o | u  i  a | e  a  o |
| e  a  o | u  o  i | a  u  i | u  a  i |
| u  a  e | o  e  a | a  e  o | o  e  i |
| u  e  a | a  o  i | u  e  a | e  o  i |

Color each box by the code.

| a = blue    e = green    i = red    o = yellow    u = orange |
|---|

Name _____

## Groundhog Groups

Which groundhogs belong together?
Name each picture.  Color by the code.

> If a word begins with *ch*, color it **brown**.
> If a word begins with *sh*, color it **green**.

# VALENTINE'S DAY

No one knows exactly how Valentine's Day started, but there are several stories behind it. Some people trace it to an ancient Roman festival called *Lupercalia.* Other people connect it to one or more saints in the early Christian church named Valentine. Still others link it with an old English belief that birds choose their mates on February 14. Today Valentine's Day is a special day for remembering sweethearts, friends, and family members with cards, candy, or gifts.

## Heart-To-Heart Conversation

Your students will really take this writing assignment to heart! Distribute a copy of "Conversation Starter" on page 12 to each child. Then give each child several large candy conversation hearts. Ask him to select five pieces to glue on his paper where indicated. (The remaining candy hearts can be eaten to make this assignment extrasweet.) Instruct each child to write a valentine story that includes some or all of the candies' phrases. Display the stories for an extrasweet reading treat!

## Special Delivery

Let your students experience the joy of giving with these special-delivery valentine cards. Give each child a copy of one card pattern from page 15 and an envelope pattern from page 16. (Have extra copies of each ready for students who would like to make more cards.) To make a card, have each child write the recipient's name and her own name; then have her color and cut out her card. Have each child write the same recipient's name on the envelope. Then have her complete the envelope by folding it where indicated and gluing the folded paper along the sides. The long unfolded side should remain unglued. When the glue is dry, have each student tuck her card inside the envelope and deliver it. Parents, friends, sitters, and other special people will love receiving these special Valentine wishes from your students!

## Heart Connections

Pair students for partner activities using this interactive game. In advance sort candy conversation hearts to form pairs of matching phrases. Find enough candy pairs so that each child will have one candy heart. Give each child a conversation heart; then instruct him to move throughout the classroom calling out the phrase. When students with matching phrases find each other, have them sit together. After you confirm that their phrases are a match, have them eat their candy and listen for directions to a partner activity of your choice.

Name _____

## Sweetheart Blends
Write each missing blend.
Find the words in the puzzle.

____uck

____ed

____ock

____um

____ab

| c | l | o | c | k | r | t |
|---|---|---|---|---|---|---|
| r | v | s | d | r | u | m |
| a | j | f | r | o | g | s |
| b | s | l | e | d | k | n |
| j | t | a | s | f | h | a |
| m | a | g | s | p | a | i |
| t | r | u | c | k | p | l |

____ag

____ail

____ar

____og

____ess

# Tower Of Valentines

Subtract.
Color each heart with a matching answer.

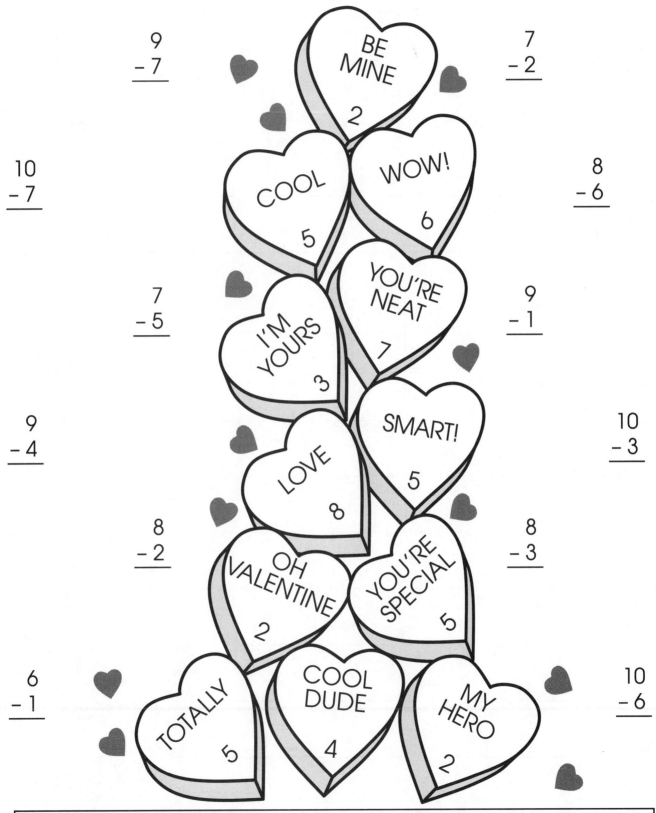

$$\begin{array}{r} 9 \\ -7 \\ \hline \end{array}$$

$$\begin{array}{r} 7 \\ -2 \\ \hline \end{array}$$

$$\begin{array}{r} 10 \\ -7 \\ \hline \end{array}$$

$$\begin{array}{r} 8 \\ -6 \\ \hline \end{array}$$

$$\begin{array}{r} 7 \\ -5 \\ \hline \end{array}$$

$$\begin{array}{r} 9 \\ -1 \\ \hline \end{array}$$

$$\begin{array}{r} 9 \\ -4 \\ \hline \end{array}$$

$$\begin{array}{r} 10 \\ -3 \\ \hline \end{array}$$

$$\begin{array}{r} 8 \\ -2 \\ \hline \end{array}$$

$$\begin{array}{r} 8 \\ -3 \\ \hline \end{array}$$

$$\begin{array}{r} 6 \\ -1 \\ \hline \end{array}$$

$$\begin{array}{r} 10 \\ -6 \\ \hline \end{array}$$

BE MINE 2
COOL 5
WOW! 6
YOU'RE NEAT 7
I'M YOURS 3
SMART! 5
LOVE 8
OH VALENTINE 2
YOU'RE SPECIAL 5
TOTALLY 5
COOL DUDE 4
MY HERO 2

**Bonus Box:** On the back of this sheet, write a sentence using the words from a heart.

Name _____

# Conversation Starter

Glue your candy hearts here.

Use the words to write a story.

_____

_____

_____

_____

_____

_____

_____

_____

_____

_____

**Note To The Teacher:** Use with "Heart-To-Heart Conversation" on page 9.

Name _____

Cut and glue to match.

## "Valen-Time"

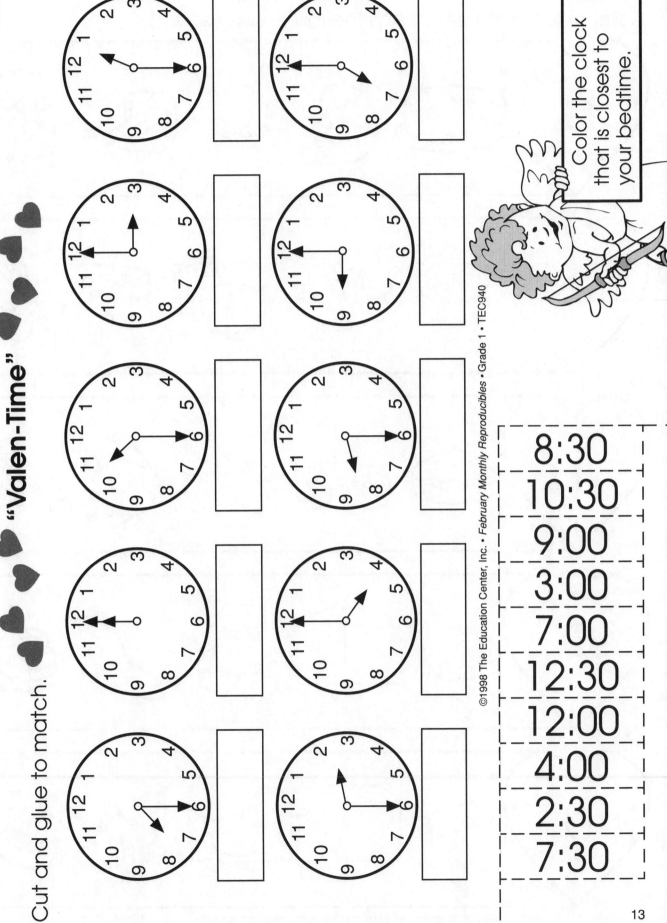

Color the clock that is closest to your bedtime.

| 8:30 |
|------|
| 10:30 |
| 9:00 |
| 3:00 |
| 7:00 |
| 12:30 |
| 12:00 |
| 4:00 |
| 2:30 |
| 7:30 |

# Valentine Vowels

Color each picture that has the long vowel sound.

# Cute Cards

You make me
smile!

To: _____

From: _____

©1998 The Education Center, Inc.

You're a purr-fect
Valentine!

To: _____

From: _____

©1998 The Education Center, Inc.

**Note To The Teacher:** Use with "Special Delivery" on page 9 and the envelope on page 16.

To: _____

From: _____

↑
Fold.

**Note To The Teacher:** Use with "Special Delivery" on page 9 and "Cute Cards" on page 15.

# Black History Month

The history and heritage of Black Americans are significant elements in the development of the United States. Much of the culture we know today has developed from events, discoveries, and actions of Black Americans. Take your students on a journey beginning with legendary Black American heroes and ending with present-day role models. They'll soon appreciate what an important influence Black Americans were and continue to be in our country.

## Flashbacks

Black History Month provides an exciting opportunity to introduce your students to some significant Black Americans. Have your students describe the impact of these important people through pictures. Distribute a copy of "Looking Back" (on page 22) to each child. Ask each child to think of a way his life has changed thanks to a Black American he has learned about. Have him draw what life was like during that person's lifetime in the first box. Then have him draw how his life is now thanks to the impact of that person. Finally, have each child write the name of the person whose life impressed him. This activity can be done as a whole class each time a significant Black American is discussed; or, after studying the impacts of several Black Americans, have each child choose one person to feature. The following list suggests just a few who could be featured:

Mary McLeod Bethune

- Benjamin Banneker
- Sojourner Truth
- Frederick Douglass
- Harriet Tubman
- Booker T. Washington
- Mary McLeod Bethune
- Marian Anderson
- Jackie Robinson
- Martin Luther King, Jr.

Booker T. Washington

## Heritage Gala

After studying several significant Black Americans throughout history, honor them with a heritage gala. Create a fairlike atmosphere with student-run booths. Each booth should highlight a person or an accomplishment that recognizes important Black Americans. Encourage students to make posters or projects, write stories, or design costumes to decorate their booths. Enlist parents' or community members' help to provide snacks that reflect African tradition. Invite students, parents, and community members to visit the display. What an honorable event!

Elijah McCoy

# Great Ideas!

Great inventors throughout history have provided us with the basis for many of the conveniences we enjoy today. Many of these innovative ideas came from Black Americans. Despite the constraints of prejudice, these great men and women developed and introduced their great ideas. Share just a few of these inventions by giving each student a copy of page 19. Have each child cut along the heavy solid outline; then have her fold on the dotted lines to form a minibook. Ask each child to write her name on the cover of the booklet. Discuss each person's invention and share the date that the patent was issued. Then have your students draw modern-day versions of each invention on the appropriate pages.

# Stars Of African-American History

Encourage your youngsters to honor their favorite "stars" in Black history by creating a stand-up star display. Through literature, media, and other means, introduce your students to the contributions of significant Black Americans. Give each child a construction-paper copy of the pattern on page 20. Ask her to select one Black American whom she feels deserves star recognition; then have her write the person's name on the first line. Have her complete the sentence telling why that person should be recognized. Ask each child to draw a picture in the star to show about the special contribution her "star" made. To display, have each child cut on the solid outline and fold the paper back on the two broken lines. Set the stars on a table with a banner reading "Our Stars Of Black American History!"

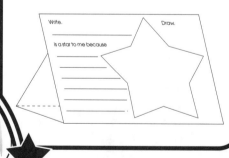

# Proud To Be Me

Black Americans have faced prejudice since the first Africans reached America in the early 1600s—causing many to become strong and independent. Discuss individualism by creating this bulletin board that celebrates diversity. In the process, you will help your students understand that prejudices can be overcome. Distribute a copy of page 21 to each child and have him complete a "Proud To Be Me" poem. (If a child does not have siblings, have him write the names of pets or friends for line five.) Ask each child to cut out his poem along the heavy solid outline. Mount the collection on a prominent bulletin board.

Sojourner Truth

② ①

Draw.

Draw.

John Standard
invented the refrigerator.

Alexander Miles
invented the elevator.

1891

1887

---

1892

_____'s

**Sarah Boone**

invented the ironing board.

**Book About**
**Black American**
**Inventors**

Draw.

③

**Note To The Teacher:** Use with "Great Ideas!" on page 18. (John Standard is listed as John Stanard in some references.)

Write.

Draw.

____________________________________

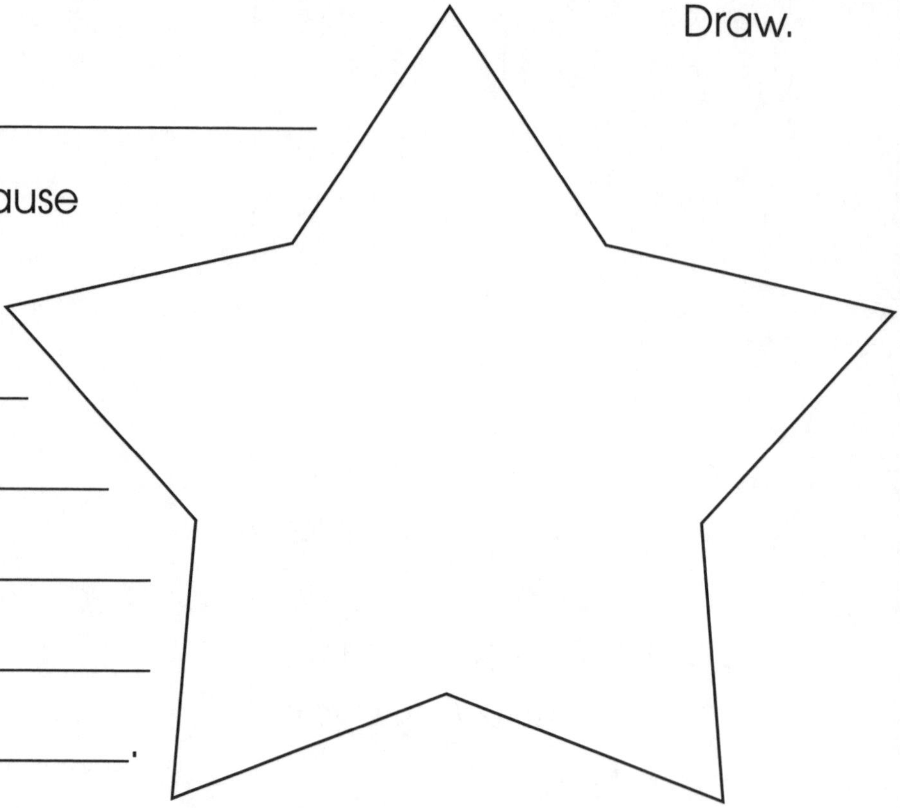

is a star to me because

__________________

_____________________

_________________________

___________________________

___________________________

___________________________.



Fold back.

Fold back.

Name ____________________________________

©1998 The Education Center, Inc. • *February Monthly Reproducibles* • Grade 1 • TEC940

 **Note To The Teacher:** Use with "Stars Of African-American History" on page 18.

# Proud To Be Me

Write.

• your first name _____

• two words that tell about you _____

• two things you like _____

• two things you don't like _____

• the names of your brothers and sisters _____

• the names of your parents _____

• your birthday _____

• your last name _____

**Note To The Teacher:** Use with "Proud To Be Me" on page 18.

## Looking Back

Think about the past. Think about today.
Draw.

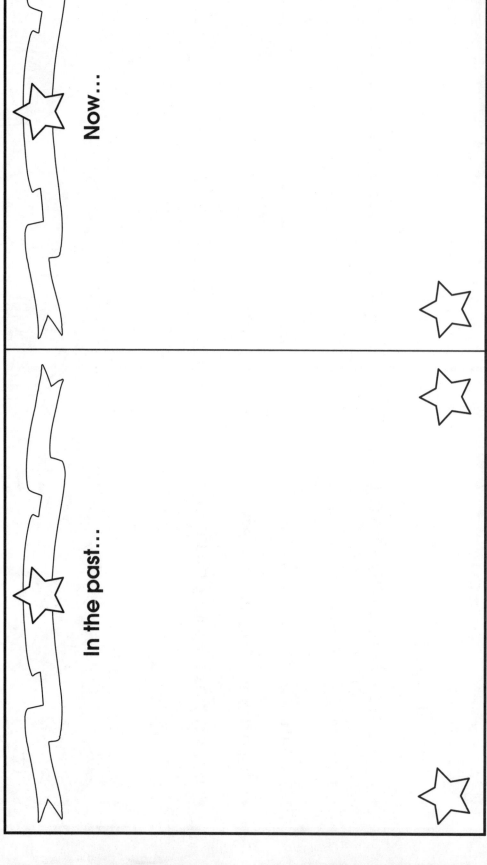

In the past...

Now...

Write. _____

Thank you, _____.

©1998 The Education Center, Inc. • *February Monthly Reproducibles* • Grade 1 • TEC940

**Note To The Teacher:** Use with "Flashbacks" on page 17.

# CHINESE NEW YEAR

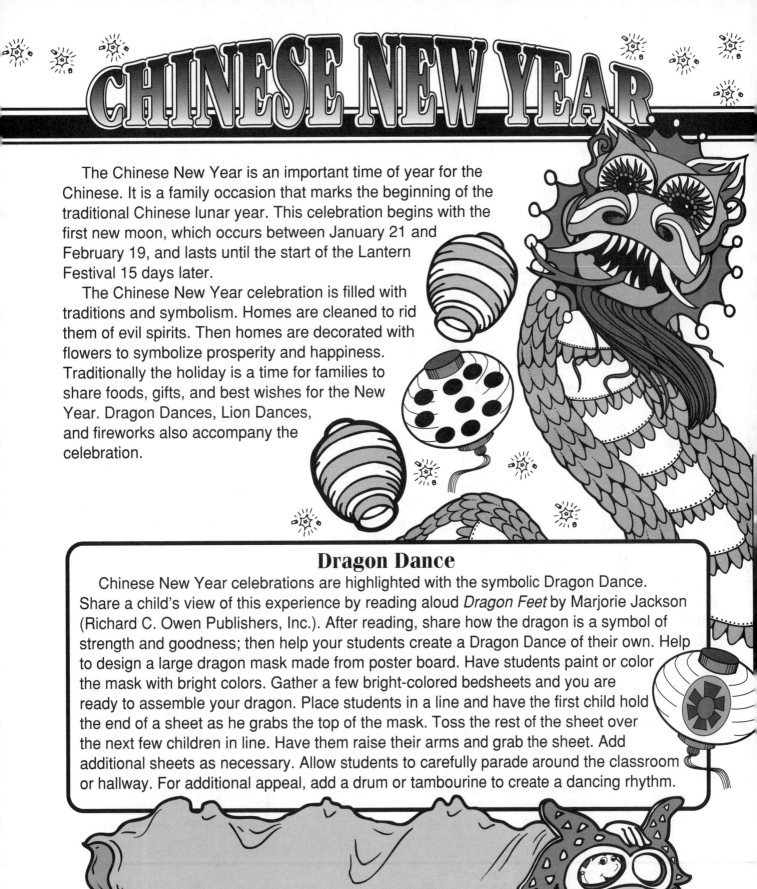

The Chinese New Year is an important time of year for the Chinese. It is a family occasion that marks the beginning of the traditional Chinese lunar year. This celebration begins with the first new moon, which occurs between January 21 and February 19, and lasts until the start of the Lantern Festival 15 days later.

The Chinese New Year celebration is filled with traditions and symbolism. Homes are cleaned to rid them of evil spirits. Then homes are decorated with flowers to symbolize prosperity and happiness. Traditionally the holiday is a time for families to share foods, gifts, and best wishes for the New Year. Dragon Dances, Lion Dances, and fireworks also accompany the celebration.

## Dragon Dance

Chinese New Year celebrations are highlighted with the symbolic Dragon Dance. Share a child's view of this experience by reading aloud *Dragon Feet* by Marjorie Jackson (Richard C. Owen Publishers, Inc.). After reading, share how the dragon is a symbol of strength and goodness; then help your students create a Dragon Dance of their own. Help to design a large dragon mask made from poster board. Have students paint or color the mask with bright colors. Gather a few bright-colored bedsheets and you are ready to assemble your dragon. Place students in a line and have the first child hold the end of a sheet as he grabs the top of the mask. Toss the rest of the sheet over the next few children in line. Have them raise their arms and grab the sheet. Add additional sheets as necessary. Allow students to carefully parade around the classroom or hallway. For additional appeal, add a drum or tambourine to create a dancing rhythm.

# Happy New Year!

Imagine comparing your personality traits to animal characteristics. Sound unique? That's just what the Chinese Fortune Calendar does. The 12-year calendar features characteristics of 12 animals which are then linked to the year when a person was born. Use the chart below to determine your students' traits based on their birth years. Then give each child a copy of "New Year Names" on page 25. After each child completes the page, have him color the animal that represents his birth year.

| 1990 | Year of the Horse | hardworking, talented, cheerful, popular |
| 1991 | Year of the Sheep | artistic, caring, trusting, wise |
| 1992 | Year of the Monkey | funny, curious, mischievous, energetic |
| 1993 | Year of the Rooster | aggressive, determined, talented, affectionate |
| 1994 | Year of the Dog | loyal, generous, trusted, sympathetic |
| 1995 | Year of the Pig | brave, caring, naive, jolly |
| 1996 | Year of the Rat | charming, fair, popular, inventive |
| 1997 | Year of the Ox | strong, stubborn, dependable, honest |
| 1998 | Year of the Tiger | brave, kind, aggressive, respected |
| 1999 | Year of the Rabbit | bright, pleasant, independent, humble |
| 2000 | Year of the Dragon | flashy, bold, decisive, elegant |
| 2001 | Year of the Snake | admired, sneaky, pushy, subtle |

## Light The Way

A traditional ending to the Chinese New Year festival includes a lantern parade. Involve your students in a similar celebration by having them create lanterns of their own. Give each child a copy of "Lantern Light" on page 26; use the directions listed here to help her complete her lantern project.

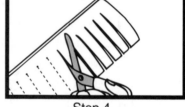
Step 4

**How To Use Page 26 To Make A Chinese Lantern**
1. Have each child color the dragon design.
2. Have each child cut out the lantern and handle patterns along the heavy solid outlines.
3. Instruct each student to fold the paper lengthwise and hold the paper so the broken cutting lines are facing her.
4. Have each student cut on the broken lines, stopping at each dot.
5. Ask each child to unfold her paper and place a line of glue where indicated. Have her bend the paper around and press the short ends together until the glue dries.
6. Instruct each child to put glue on each end of the handle and attach it as shown.

Step 5

Step 6

# New Year Names

Write each animal's name. Use the word box.

| | 1990 | | 1996 |
|---|---|---|---|
| | 1991 | | 1997 |
| | 1992 | | 1998 |
| | 1993 | | 1999 |
| | 1994 | | 2000 |
| | 1995 | | 2001 |

## Word Box

| ox | monkey | horse | pig |
|---|---|---|---|
| tiger | dragon | dog | rabbit |
| rooster | sheep | rat | snake |

**Note To The Teacher:** Use with "Happy New Year!" on page 24.

# Lantern Light

Listen and do.

| Glue here. | Fold. | Glue here. | Glue. |

©1998 The Education Center, Inc. • *February Monthly Reproducibles* • Grade 1 • TEC940

**Note To The Teacher:** Use with "Light The Way" on page 24.

# PRESIDENTS' DAY

Presidents' Day was originally declared to celebrate the birthdays of Presidents George Washington (born February 22, 1732) and Abraham Lincoln (born February 12, 1809). President Washington is best remembered for being the first president and the "father of our country." President Lincoln, our 16th president, is known for his strong leadership during the Civil War years and for freeing the slaves. As we pay tribute to both men on the third Monday in February, it is also a time to honor all the presidents of the United States.

**U.S. Presidents**

1. George Washington
2. John Adams
3. Thomas Jefferson
4. James Madison
5. James Monroe
6. John Quincy Adams
7. Andrew Jackson
8. Martin Van Buren
9. William H. Harrison
10. John Tyler
11. James K. Polk
12. Zachary Taylor
13. Millard Fillmore
14. Franklin Pierce
15. James Buchanan
16. Abraham Lincoln
17. Andrew Johnson
18. Ulysses S. Grant
19. Rutherford B. Hayes
20. James A. Garfield
21. Chester A. Arthur
22. Grover Cleveland
23. Benjamin Harrison
24. Grover Cleveland
25. William McKinley
26. Theodore Roosevelt
27. William H. Taft
28. Woodrow Wilson
29. Warren G. Harding
30. Calvin Coolidge
31. Herbert C. Hoover
32. Franklin D. Roosevelt
33. Harry S. Truman
34. Dwight D. Eisenhower
35. John F. Kennedy
36. Lyndon B. Johnson
37. Richard M. Nixon
38. Gerald R. Ford
39. James E. Carter
40. Ronald W. Reagan
41. George H. W. Bush
42. William J. Clinton

## Presidential Presentation

Presidents' Day is the perfect time to introduce your students to several U.S. leaders and share their accomplishments. Using the list on this page, assign each child one of our past presidents. Provide each student with a brief profile (dates in office, significant accomplishment, family information, etc.) about his assigned president. Help each child read the information; then ask him to draw a picture representing what he learned about the president. Conclude the lesson by having each child present his information and his picture to his classmates; then display the posters in sequential order for all to view.

# Fraction Hat

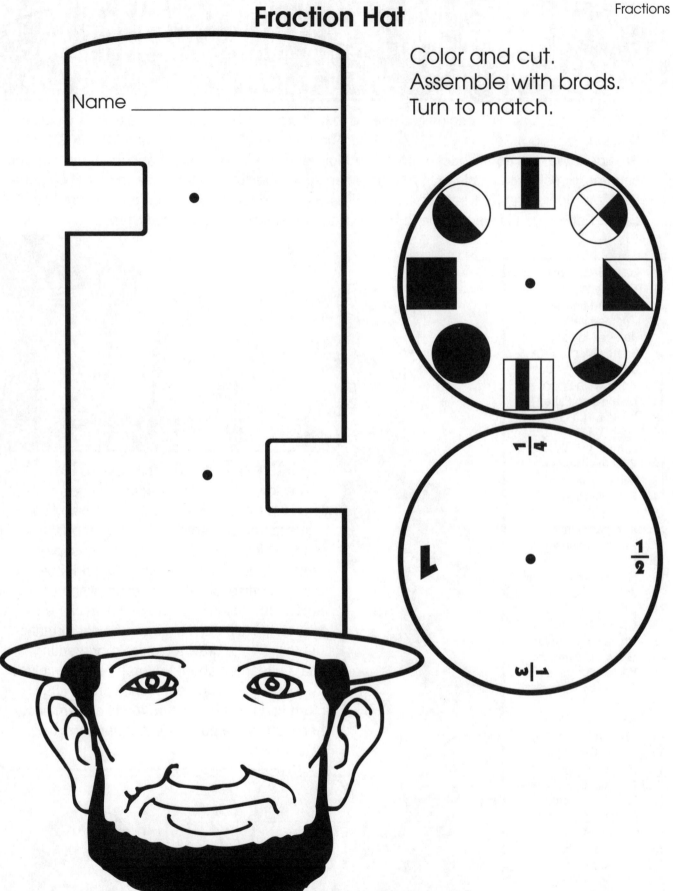

Name _____

Color and cut.
Assemble with brads.
Turn to match.

**Note To The Teacher:** Duplicate on white construction paper.

Name _____

# Presidential Plurals

Cut and glue to match.

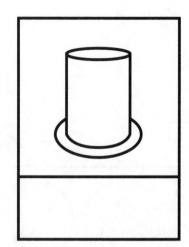

| tree | hat | book | horses |
|------|-----|------|--------|
| books | horse | trees | hats |

Name_____

# Presidents' Coin Collection

## Count the coins. Color the matching amount.

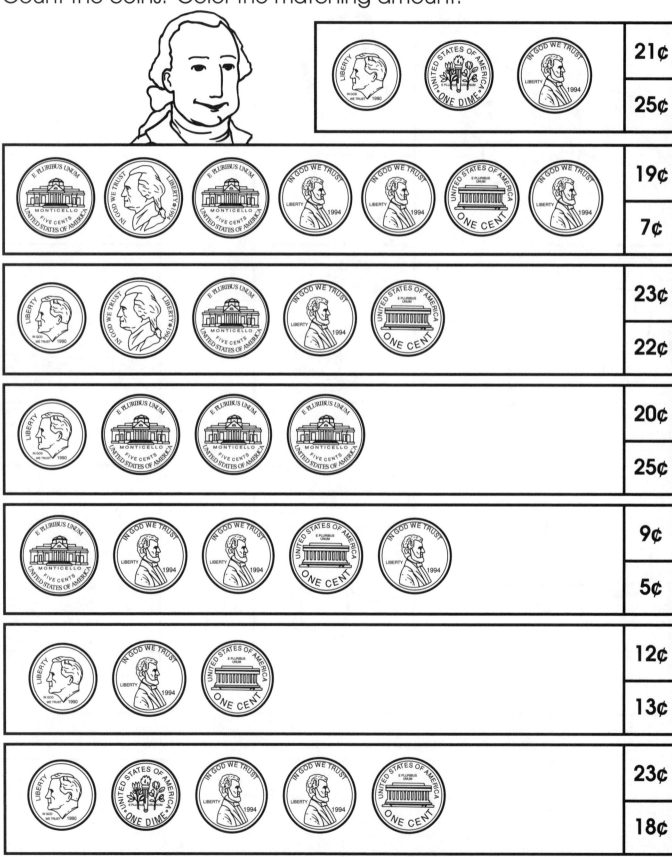

| | |
|---|---|
| 21¢ | 25¢ |
| 19¢ | 7¢ |
| 23¢ | 22¢ |
| 20¢ | 25¢ |
| 9¢ | 5¢ |
| 12¢ | 13¢ |
| 23¢ | 18¢ |

Name_____

# Add It Up, Abe!

```
   3        5        6        1
   4        1        1        2
 + 1      + 4      + 2      + 3
 ___      ___      ___      ___


   4        8        3        2
   4        2        1        7
 + 2      + 2      + 5      + 1
 ___      ___      ___      ___


   7        2        1        9
   4        3        9        0
 + 0      + 5      + 2      + 3
 ___      ___      ___      ___


            8        5        4
            3        5        2
          + 1      + 0      + 6
          ___      ___      ___
```

**Bonus Box:** On the back of this sheet, add your age and the ages of 2 friends.

# Punctuating Presidents

A telling sentence ends with a **period.**

An asking sentence ends with a **question mark.**

Write a **?** or **.**

1.  George Washington was born in February _____

2.  Did Abe Lincoln live in a log cabin _____

3.  Abe liked to read books _____

4.  When do we celebrate Presidents' Day _____

5.  Who was the first president _____

6.  Abe was an honest man _____

7.  George liked to ride horses _____

8.  Which president's face is on a penny _____

9.  Who signed the Declaration of Independence _____

10. Abe Lincoln grew a beard _____

# FAIRY TALES

Tales of elves, witches, princes, and princesses have long entertained generations of children. Perhaps the most well-known of these tales were collected by two German brothers, Jacob and Wilhelm Grimm. The Grimm brothers published more than 200 tales, including "Hansel And Gretel," "Little Red Riding Hood," "Sleeping Beauty," and "The Elves And The Shoemaker." Both brothers devoted much of their lives to retelling and preserving German tales, but their later editions were compiled primarily by Wilhelm, who was born on February 24, 1786. Honor these famous authors in February by studying their enchanting fairy tales with your students.

## Character Comparison

Engage youngsters in this character study that's beyond compare! First share with students James Marshall's humorous version of *Red Riding Hood* (Puffin Books, 1993). Next draw four columns on your chalkboard. Have students name the main characters in this fairy tale and write each of the character's names at the top of a separate column. Challenge students to brainstorm traits that describe each of these characters and record youngsters' ideas below the corresponding column headings. Encourage students to identify the story information that supports each of the named attributes. Discuss with youngsters the similarities and differences among the characters; then give each child a copy of the reproducible on page 34 to follow up this discussion. Now that's a "tale-or-made" character study!

## Tell The Story

Give letter writing a fanciful twist with this creative activity. Read aloud your favorite version of "Sleeping Beauty"; then review the story's sequence of events with students. Invite each youngster to write a letter to Sleeping Beauty telling her about the spell and explaining what happened while she was asleep. Remind each student to include the date, a greeting, a closing, and her signature in her letter. Invite youngsters to read aloud their completed letters to the class. Next have each student reinforce her sequencing skills by completing a copy of the reproducible on page 35. No doubt students will enjoy this spellbinding language-arts lesson!

## Fabulous Fairy Tales

Look for these popular titles by the Grimm brothers.
*The Elves And The Shoemaker* by Bernadette Watts (North-South Books Inc., 1997)
*Rapunzel* by Carol Heyer (Hambleton-Hill Publishing, Inc.; 1995)
*The Bremen Town Musicians* by Janet Stevens (Holiday House, Inc.; 1992)
*Snow White And Rose Red* by Bernadette Watts (North-South Books Inc., 1997)

Name _____

# Character Matchup

Cut. Glue to match.

| Red Riding Hood | The Wolf | Granny | The Hunter |
|---|---|---|---|
| | | | |
| | | | |

©1998 The Education Center, Inc. • *February Monthly Reproducibles* • Grade 1 • TEC940

| He helped Red Riding Hood. | She rested in bed. | She visited Granny. | He tricked Granny. |
|---|---|---|---|
| He was mean. | She took a walk. | He saved Granny. | She was sick. |

**Note To The Teacher:** Use with "Character Comparison" on page 33.

# Tell The Story

Cut and glue to tell the story.

| | | | |
|---|---|---|---|
| 1 | 2 | 3 | 4 |

## Read. Write a number to show the order.

☐ She fell asleep.

☐ A woman cast a spell.

☐ A prince kissed her.

☐ The girl pricked her finger.

## Write a sentence that tells what happened next.

_____

_____

_____

_____

_____

**Note To The Teacher:** Use with "Tell The Story" on page 33.

# Royal Sums

Add. Cut. Glue.

| | | | | |
|---|---|---|---|---|
| 5 + 5 = _____ | 4 + 8 = _____ | 5 + 7 = _____ | 9 + 3 = _____ | 3 + 8 = _____ |
| 4 + 6 = _____ | 9 + 2 = _____ | 3 + 7 = _____ | 5 + 6 = _____ | 7 + 4 = _____ |

Name_____

# Enchanted Forest

Read.  Color.

What is north of  ?   orange

What is east of  ?  green

What is west of 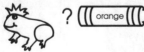 ?  purple

What is south of  ?  blue

What is north of  ?  red

**Bonus Box:** On the back of this sheet, draw and color a map of your classroom.

**Note To The Teacher:** Have students color a building to answer each question.

Name _____

38

## Shoes By Twos

How many shoes are on each shelf? Count by 2s. Write.

| | | | | | Total ____ |
|---|---|---|---|---|---|
| | | | | | Total ____ |
| | | | | | Total ____ |
| | | | | | Total ____ |

**Bonus Box:** If you have 20 pairs of shoes, how many shoes do you have? Write your answer on the back of this sheet.

**Note To The Teacher:** Read aloud "The Elves And The Shoemaker" to introduce this lesson.

# FUN WITH CLIFFORD

Who's big and red and ready to pounce on you with an abundance of reading fun? That's right! Clifford! February 15 marks the birthday of Norman Bridwell, the creator of this adorable, larger-than-life pet. So roll out the red carpet for this special dog and his creator this month. After hearing these fun tales and trying these activities, your students will be beggin' for more!

## "Write" On, Clifford!

Make writing more interesting with this adorable Clifford paper topper. Begin by having each child write an original story using one of the writing topics on this page. Then give each child a copy of page 42. Demonstrate how to color, cut, and assemble the project to create a dandy writing display. Mount all of the finished projects on a bulletin board titled " 'Write' On, Clifford!"

## Stories Galore

With dozens of Clifford stories to choose from, everyone will find a favorite. Here are just a few to get you started, all published by Scholastic Inc.

*Clifford At The Circus,* 1985
*Clifford Takes A Trip,* 1985
*Clifford The Big Red Dog,* 1988
*Clifford's Family,* 1984
*Clifford's Kitten,* 1984
*Clifford's Pals,* 1985

### Writing Topics

- Tell why you want Clifford to live at your house.
- Make up a new ending to a favorite Clifford story.
- Describe how things would be different if Clifford were tiny.
- Create a new Clifford adventure.
- Describe a typical meal for Clifford.
- Tell about Clifford's toys.

# Book Bones

Read a story about Clifford.
Write.

**Title:**

_____

**Main Characters:**

_____

_____        _____

**Setting:**

_____

**Main Event:**

_____

_____

_____

**Note To The Teacher:** Some suggested titles can be found on page 39.

Name _____

# Clifford Capers

Help Clifford solve these story problems.
Read each sentence.
Add or subtract.
Write your answer.

| | | |
|---|---|---|
| Clifford chewed 3 shoes.<br>He chewed 2 more.<br>How many in all?<br><br>3 + 2 = 5<br><br>⬚ 5 shoes | Clifford saw 6 cars.<br>He saw 1 more.<br>How many in all?<br><br><br>⬚ cars | Clifford had 8 bones.<br>He ate 3.<br>How many are left?<br><br><br>⬚ bones |
| Clifford dug up 5 flowers.<br>He dug up 4 more.<br>How many in all?<br><br><br>⬚ flowers | 7 birds landed.<br>Clifford chased 3 away.<br>How many are left?<br><br><br>⬚ birds | Clifford saw 3 cats.<br>He saw 4 more.<br>How many in all?<br><br><br>⬚ cats |
| Clifford did 3 tricks.<br>He did 3 more.<br>How many did he do?<br><br><br>⬚ tricks | Clifford had 4 bowls of water.<br>He drank 2.<br>How many are left?<br><br><br>⬚ bowls | 9 friends pet Clifford.<br>1 more pet him.<br>How many in all?<br><br><br>⬚ friends |

# Clifford Is Tops

Write a story about Clifford.
Color the dog.
Cut and glue him to your writing paper.

Clifford has a funny nose. It smells strange things.

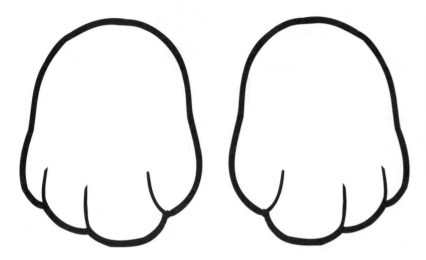

# National CHILDREN'S DENTAL HEALTH Month

February has arrived, and it's time to talk teeth. National Children's Dental Health Month was established by the American Dental Association to promote healthy habits and attitudes regarding oral health. Beginning as a one-day event on February 3, 1941, this now month-long observance provides plenty of time to talk to your students about proper tooth care.

## Tooth Topics

Your students will love brushing up on current skills with this practical activity. Make one copy of "Time For A Checkup" (see page 44) and program it using one of the following suggestions. Then make a class supply of the programmed page to distribute to your students. This is one review your students will really sink their teeth into!

### Programming Suggestions

- Write an addition or a subtraction problem on each tooth. Have each child solve the problems.

- Write a spelling word on each tooth. Have each student use the page for review.

- Write a word on each tooth and hide matching objects in the room. Then conduct a tooth treasure hunt. Have each child hunt for each item and color in the tooth as each object is found.

- Write the two components of a contraction at the top of each tooth. Have students write the corresponding contraction at the bottom of each tooth.

- Number each tooth and write a vocabulary word on it. Ask each child to write a sentence using each word on the back of his sheet.

## Sensible Snacks

Emphasize the importance of dental health by sharing some healthful snacks. Snacks such as nuts, raw vegetables, crackers, popcorn, and cheese are sure to make your students smile. Turn these treats into real crowd pleasers with a little imagination. Place a dab of peanut butter and a caulifloweret at the end of a long celery or carrot stick to create a "toothbrush." Or design a "smiling mouth" using cheese and nuts. Delicious!

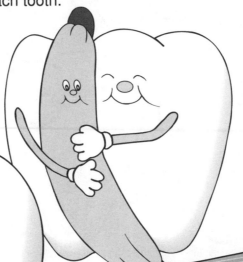

Open

# Time For A Checkup

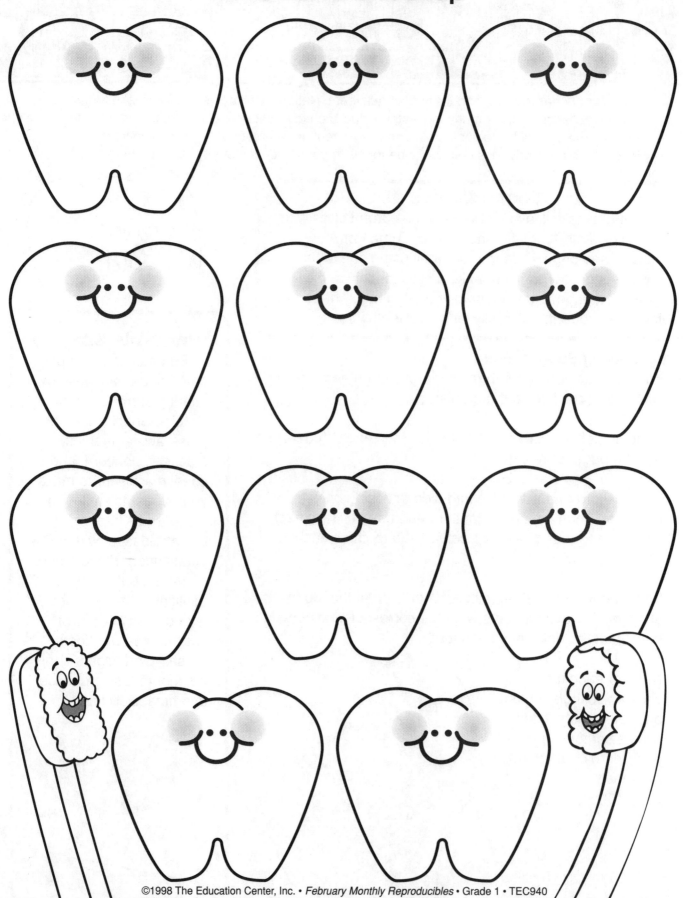

**Note To The Teacher:** For suggestions on using this page see "Tooth Topics" on page 43.

## Brushing Up!

Cut and glue to make compound words.

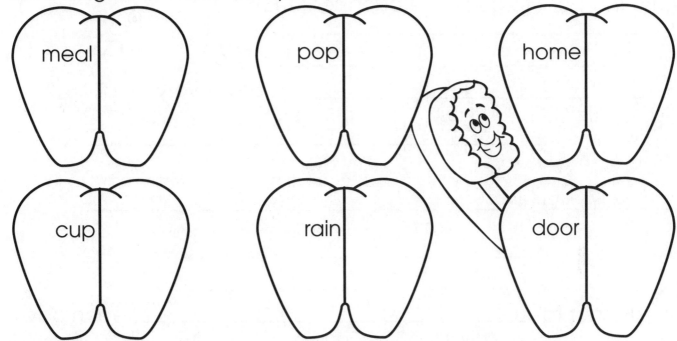

Write to make compound words. Use the word bank.

_____
## tooth

_____
## out

_____
## rain

_____
## side

**Word Bank**

side

bow

walk

paste

work    coat    time    corn    bell    cake

Name_____

## Tooth Tips

Read the sentences.
Write the word to complete each sentence.

_____

1. _____ after every meal.

      Blush        Brush        Brag

_____

2. Eat healthful _____.

      snaps      snacks      sleds

_____

3. Use dental _____ each day.

      flower      flag      floss

_____

4. Have a dentist _____ your teeth.

      clean      clam      crop

_____

5. Show off your _____.

      smart      smile      slide

Write each beginning blend.

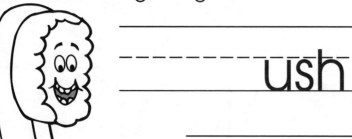

ush

oss

# NATIONAL SNACK FOOD MONTH

A child's food choices affect his mental and physical well-being. Children who have balanced, nutritious diets are generally more alert and physically healthy than youngsters who eat foods with low nutritional value. Healthful diets provide high energy, facilitate strong school performances, and increase resistance to illness. This month set the stage for a lifetime of good eating habits by teaching students about nutrition and promoting healthful snack foods.

## "Sense-ational" Snacks

Students may not realize that taste is only one of the senses they use when they eat. To demonstrate, give each student an apple wedge. Challenge each youngster to describe his apple with as many different adjectives as he can—without eating it. For example, the apple may smell sweet, feel smooth, and look shiny. List students' responses on the chalkboard. Invite each student to eat his apple wedge; then ask students to add to the list of adjectives. After the list is complete, have students identify the corresponding sense for each adjective. Follow up the activity by asking each student to write about his favorite nutritious snack. Encourage youngsters to include descriptive words that tell how the snack looks, feels, smells, tastes, and if applicable, sounds. Students will surely develop a taste for writing with this tantalizing activity!

## Healthful Handfuls

All students can lend a hand to make this simple and nutritious snack! Give each student a small resealable plastic bag. Have her use the bag to bring to school one cup of a healthful snack that has small pieces, such as dry cereal, raisins, nuts, or pretzels. Be sure to encourage children to choose nutritious snacks. When everyone has brought in a snack, combine all of the treats in a large bowl. Give each child a portion; then have her create a graph to show the amount and type of each ingredient in her portion. Display the completed graphs for all to see, and ask students to compare them. Of what ingredient do students have the most? The least? Do all portions have the same ingredients? Not only will students learn about nutritious snacks and improve their math skills, they'll savor the benefits of teamwork too!

## Pack A Snack

Students will have food for thought when they create this nutritious snack display! In advance make a large bulletin-board-paper cutout that resembles a lunchbox. Have students brainstorm healthful snacks as you record their ideas on the chalkboard. Then ask each student to cut out a picture of a nutritious snack from a discarded magazine. Direct each youngster to glue his picture onto the lunchbox cutout. After each youngster has added a picture, mount the resulting collage on a brightly colored bulletin board. With this appetizing display, students will be on track with smart snacks!

## Tasty Titles

*The Berenstain Bears And Too Much Junk Food* by Stan and Jan Berenstain (Random House Books For Young Readers, 1985)

*What Food Is This?* by Rosmarie Hausherr (Scholastic Inc., 1994)

*The Edible Pyramid: Good Eating Every Day* by Loreen Leedy (Holiday House, Inc.; 1996)

Name_____ 

## A Tasty Lineup

Cut and glue the words in ABC order.

| |
|:---:|
| **1** |
| **2** |
| **3** |
| **4** |
| **5** |
| **6** |
| **7** |
| **8** |
| **9** |
| **10** |

carrot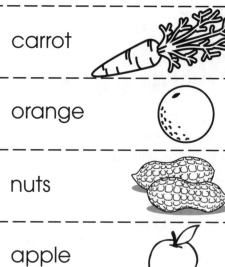

orange

nuts

apple

juice

pear

grapes

milk

banana

raisins

**Bonus Box:** On the back of your paper, write three other nutritious snacks in ABC order.

Name _____

# Jack's Snack

Read each box.
Add or subtract.

| | |
|---|---|
| Jack has 4  s.<br><br>He gets 9 more.<br><br>He has ☐  s in all. | Jack has 13  s.<br><br>He eats 3.<br><br>He has ☐ s left. |
| Jack has 12  .<br><br>He drops 7.<br><br>He has ☐  left. | Jack has 10 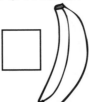 s.<br><br>He gets 3 more.<br><br>He has ☐ s in all. |
| Jack has 4  s.<br><br>He gets 9 more.<br><br>He has ☐ s in all. | Jack has 13  s.<br><br>He eats 4.<br><br>He has ☐  s left. |

**Bonus Box:** On the back of this sheet, write a story problem about another healthful snack.

Name _____

# Treats To Eat

Read the words.
Cut. Put a dot of glue on each ●.
Glue each picture onto the matching plate.
Color the healthful snacks.

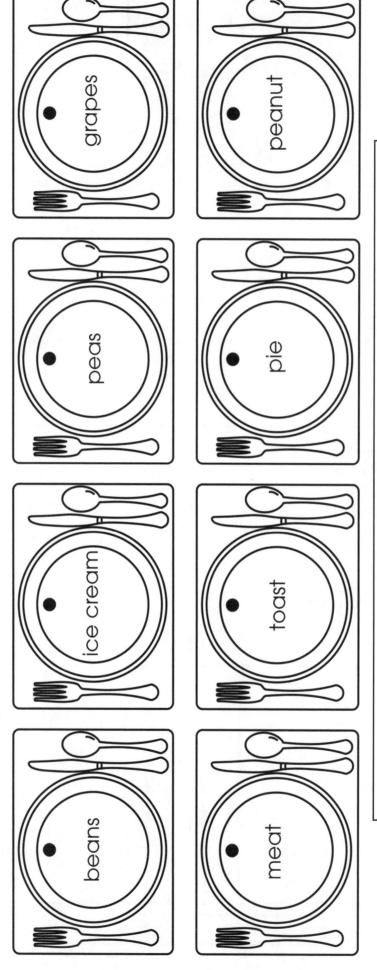

beans

ice cream

peas

grapes

meat

toast

pie

peanut

**Bonus Box:** On the back of your paper, write a sentence with one of the long e words.

©1998 The Education Center, Inc. • *February Monthly Reproducibles* • Grade 1 • TEC940

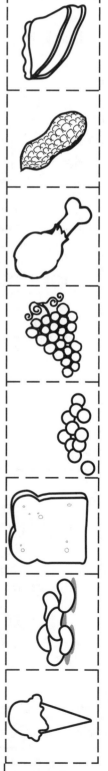

# Responsible Pet Owner Month

Studying proper pet care is the "purr-fect" way for youngsters to learn about responsibility. The American Society For The Prevention Of Cruelty To Animals sponsors this monthlong focus on exercise, grooming, nutrition, and veterinary care for pets.

## Pet "Cat-egories"

Students will have all sorts of fun with this hands-on categorization activity! Give each student a copy of the reproducible on page 52. Instruct each youngster to color and cut apart his animal picture cards. Pair students and have each twosome work in an area of the classroom where they can easily spread out the cards. Direct each child to take turns sorting his cards into categories of his choice—such as animals with fur and those without—then asking his partner to determine how the cards were sorted. Each student continues working with his partner by repeating this process. Challenge youngsters to find as many different ways to sort the animals as possible. With this activity, students' categorization skills will be picture-perfect in no time at all!

## A Perfect Pet

Unleash students' imaginations with this creative-writing idea! Read aloud *Can I Have A Stegosaurus, Mom? Can I? Please!?* by Lois G. Grambling (BridgeWater Books, 1997). This humorous story describes the surprising benefits of having a pet stegosaurus. Ask youngsters to brainstorm animals that they would like to own, including those that are not normally considered appropriate pets. Record students' ideas on the chalkboard and instruct each youngster to select one animal from the list. Then have each child write and illustrate a story explaining why her chosen animal would be a good pet. (Encourage students to use Grambling's style as a model.) After children share their completed stories with their classmates, mount their work on a brightly colored bulletin board for all to enjoy. No doubt this unusual pet menagerie will receive rave reviews!

## Pet Tales

*Can I Keep Him?* by Steven Kellogg (Dial Books For Young Readers, 1971)

*My New Kitten* by Joanna Cole (Morrow Junior Books, 1995)

*Any Kind Of Dog* by Lynn Reiser (Mulberry Books, 1994)

*Let's Get A Pet* by Harriet Ziefert (Puffin Books, 1996)

**Note To The Teacher:** Use with "Pet 'Cat-egories'" on page 51.

Name_____ 

## A Pet Story

Read. Color.

**My Cat**
I have a pet cat.
It is black and white.
My cat plays with string.
I love my cat!

Write. Use the word box.

| Word Box | | | |
|---|---|---|---|
| my | black | have | plays |

_____
- - - - - - - - - - - - - - - -
I _____ a pet cat.

_____
- - - - - - - - - - - - - - - -
It is _____ and white.

_____
- - - - - - - - - - - - - - - -
My cat _____ with string.

_____
- - - - - - - - - - - - - - - -
I love _____ cat!

**Bonus Box:** What is a good name for my cat? Write the name on the back of this sheet. Tell why you like the name.

Responsible Pet Owner Month
Long vowels

# Dinner Time!

Cut out each vowel and glue it below a matching picture.

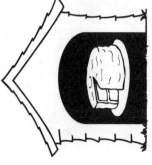

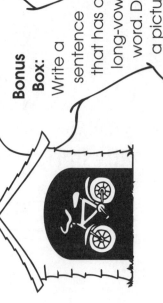

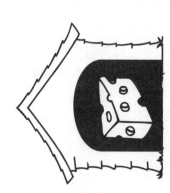

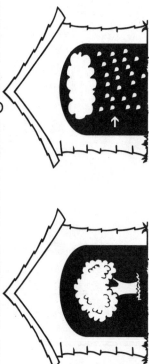

**Bonus Box:** Write a sentence that has a long-vowel word. Draw a picture to match.

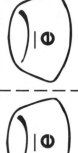

# NATIONAL PANCAKE WEEK

Students will flip over this tasty celebration! Pancake Week is observed during the week of Shrove or Pancake Tuesday (the day before Ash Wednesday). The English traditionally cook and eat flat, thin pancakes on Pancake Tuesday. Annually, since 1445, a pancake race is held in England on this day. Each competitor wears an apron and races from the marketplace to a church while carrying a pancake on a griddle.

Serve up these amazing pancake facts to students:

- The largest pancake to be flipped was cooked on February 9, 1975. It was twelve feet in diameter.

- Dominic M. Cuzzacrea ran a 26.2-mile marathon while flipping a pancake on May 6, 1990.

## Top It Off

Learn more about your students' tastes with this simple recipe for analytical thinking! Begin on Monday by asking youngsters to brainstorm their favorite pancake toppings. Record students' ideas on chart paper. Then use two of the named toppings to create a Venn diagram on the chalkboard and have each student write his name in the appropriate section. Discuss the results with youngsters and help them draw conclusions about the information shown. Use different toppings from the brainstormed list to create a Venn diagram on each of the next three days and analyze the information with students. On Friday make a Venn diagram with three toppings to provide an extra challenge for youngsters. Top off this appetizing week with a class pancake breakfast. Enlist the help of volunteers and be sure to provide a variety of favorite toppings, such as jams, syrups, powdered sugar, and peanut butter. No doubt this activity will stack up to a generous helping of fun!

### What do you like on your pancakes?

Don

Syrup — John, Kristie, Alice

Pam, Danny

Jam — Rebecca, Deanna, Nancy

Jake

## What's For Breakfast?

Some youngsters aren't aware of all the preparation involved in cooking breakfast. *Pancakes, Pancakes!* by Eric Carle (Scholastic Inc., 1992) is a delightful book about a young boy who learns this lesson firsthand. Share this story with students; then engage them in an oral retelling. Next have each child write and illustrate a story about the steps for making his own favorite breakfast. Provide an opportunity for each youngster to read aloud his completed story to the class; then display this enticing bonanza of breakfast stories for all to enjoy.

Hungry for more books about pancakes? If so, look for these popular titles:
*Cloudy With A Chance Of Meatballs* by Judi Barrett (Simon & Schuster Books Children's Division, 1982)
*Pancakes For Breakfast* by Tomie dePaola (Harcourt Brace & Company, 1978)

Name _____

# A Tall Order

How tall is each stack?
Estimate in paper clips and write.
Measure with paper clips and write.

| Estimate. | Estimate. | Estimate. | Estimate. | Estimate. |
|---|---|---|---|---|
| ___ paper clips | ___ paper clips | ___ paper clips | ___ paper clips | ___ paper clips |
| Measure. | Measure. | Measure. | Measure. | Measure. |
| ___ paper clips | ___ paper clips | ___ paper clips | ___ paper clips | ___ paper clips |

**Bonus Box:** On the back of this sheet, draw a stack of pancakes that is 7 paper clips tall.

Name

# Please Pass The Syrup!

Cut. Glue to match.

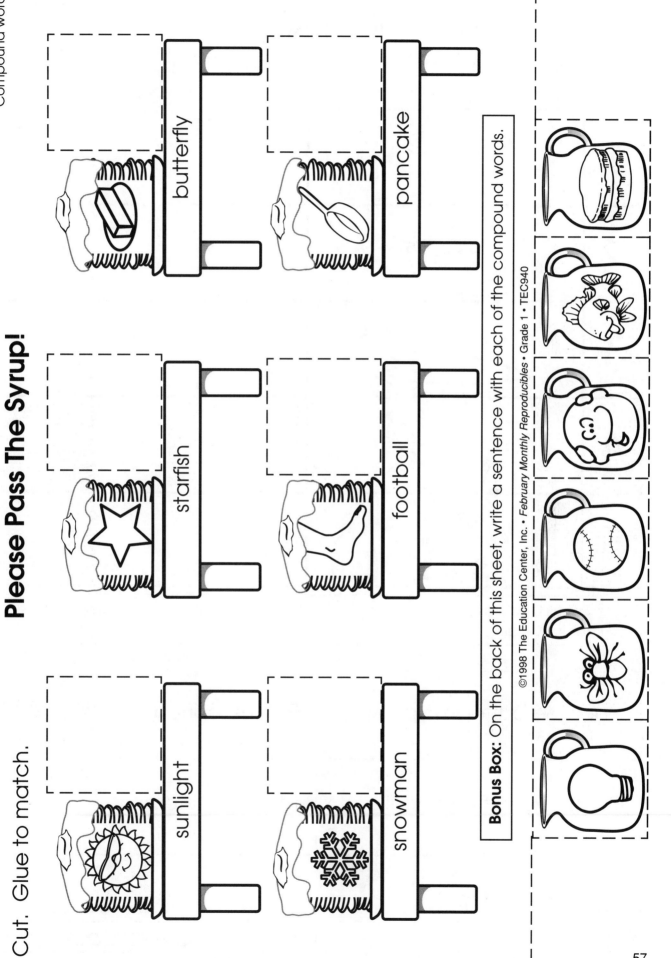

butterfly

pancake

starfish

football

sunlight

snowman

**Bonus Box:** On the back of this sheet, write a sentence with each of the compound words.

# A Great Breakfast

Cut. Glue in order.

| 1 | | |
|---|---|---|
| 2 | | |
| 3 | | |
| 4 | | |
| 5 | | |

**Bonus Box:** If one recipe makes ten pancakes, how many pancakes do three recipes make?

Cook the batter in a pan.

Put the pancake on a plate.

Cut and eat the pancake!

Mix the batter.

Put butter on top.

# International Friendship Week

Promote the importance of friendships during International Friendship Week, held the last full week of February. Use the activities in this unit to promote a caring and friendly attitude among your students as they learn more about each other.

## New Friend Day

Pair up with another teacher at your grade level to celebrate your New Friend Day. Match each student in your classroom with a student from your colleague's classroom. Then plan joint activities to last throughout the day. Begin the day by having each student write a note to introduce herself to her partner. Bring the two classes together. Have partners swap notes and introduce themselves. Next schedule a joint art, reading, or music activity. Plan a special lunch for the two classes. In the afternoon plan a game for the students to play with their new friends. Wind up the day by having each student tell about her new friend, describing what she enjoyed about the day.

## Friendship Facts

Your students will enjoy finding out just what it is about their friends that makes them so likable. Distribute a copy of page 61 to each child. Have him collect information from a friend to complete the first column. Then have the child complete the second column with his own preferences. Now it's time to compare. Do the friends have similar interests? Or do opposites attract? Follow the activity with a discussion about how friends can have similarities and differences.

## Poster Pals

Give students the opportunity to describe a perfect friend with these positive posters. Have each child design a poster showing the qualities he feels make a good friend. Encourage students to use markers, magazine clippings, and original art to make these posters especially creative.

# Friendship Fun

Write, draw, and color to finish
  each card.
Cut and punch holes.
Assemble with
  string.

FRIENDSHIP

A friend likes to

A friend should never

---

A friend likes to

---

is my kind of friend.

---

A friend should never

---

is my kind of friend.

---

# FRIENDSHIP

**Note To The Teacher:** Duplicate this page on construction or other heavy paper. Provide a hole puncher for students to use.

Name

# Friendship Facts

Survey a friend. Write.
Complete the survey yourself.
Check same or different. Compare.

| | Myself | (friend's name) | Same | Different |
|---|---|---|---|---|
| Favorite Food | | | | |
| Favorite Color | | | | |
| Favorite Game | | | | |
| Favorite School Subject | | | | |
| Favorite Story | | | | |
| Favorite Holiday | | | | |
| Favorite Pet | | | | |
| Favorite Snack | | | | |

How many are the same? _____

How many are different? _____

**Note To The Teacher:** Use with "Friendship Facts" on page 59.

# Fabulous Friends

Write a word for each letter to tell about a friend.

**F**

**R**

**I**

**E**

**N**

**D**

Write a sentence using one of the words from above.

# Math Pals

Add or subtract.

$$
\begin{array}{r} 8 \\ +4 \\ \hline \end{array}
\qquad
\begin{array}{r} 10 \\ -2 \\ \hline \end{array}
\qquad
\begin{array}{r} 9 \\ +1 \\ \hline \end{array}
\qquad
\begin{array}{r} 8 \\ -5 \\ \hline \end{array}
$$

$$
\begin{array}{r} 7 \\ +5 \\ \hline \end{array}
\qquad
\begin{array}{r} 8 \\ +2 \\ \hline \end{array}
\qquad
\begin{array}{r} 11 \\ -6 \\ \hline \end{array}
\qquad
\begin{array}{r} 10 \\ -5 \\ \hline \end{array}
$$

$$
\begin{array}{r} 12 \\ -4 \\ \hline \end{array}
\qquad
\begin{array}{r} 6 \\ +6 \\ \hline \end{array}
\qquad
\begin{array}{r} 7 \\ +2 \\ \hline \end{array}
\qquad
\begin{array}{r} 9 \\ -5 \\ \hline \end{array}
$$

$$
\begin{array}{r} 10 \\ +1 \\ \hline \end{array}
\qquad
\begin{array}{r} 11 \\ -8 \\ \hline \end{array}
$$

**Bonus Box:** Exchange papers with a friend. Check his or her work.

# Answer Keys

## Page 7

| | | | |
|---|---|---|---|
| a (blue) | e (green) | i (red) | e (green) |
| o (yellow) | u (orange) | a (blue) | u (orange) |
| e (green) | a (blue) | e (green) | o (yellow) |
| a (blue) | o (yellow) | u (orange) | i (red) |

## Page 10

**Sweetheart Blends**
Write each missing blend.
Find the words in the puzzle.

_tr_ uck

_cl_ ock

_sl_ ed

_dr_ um

_cr_ ab

_fl_ ag

_sn_ ail

_fr_ og

_st_ ar

_dr_ ess

## Page 31

| | | | |
|---|---|---|---|
| 8 | 10 | 9 | 6 |
| 10 | 12 | 9 | 10 |
| 11 | 10 | 12 | 12 |
| | 12 | 10 | 12 |

## Page 46

1. Brush
2. snacks
3. floss
4. clean
5. smile

**br**ush
**fl**oss

## Page 48

apple
banana
carrot
grapes
juice
milk
nuts
orange
pear
raisins

## Page 63

| | | | |
|---|---|---|---|
| 12 | 8 | 10 | 3 |
| 12 | 10 | 5 | 5 |
| 8 | 12 | 9 | 4 |
| 11 | 3 | | |